THE SECRET
OF
A GOOD MEMORY

THE SECRET OF A GOOD MEMORY

By

J. MORTIMER-GRANVILLE

GYAN

Published by

GYAN

Gyan Publishing House
5, Ansari Road
Daryaganj, New Delhi-110002
Phone: 011-47034999, 9811692060
E-mail: books@gyanbooks.com

Distribution Network
gyanbooks.com
India, USA, Canada, UK, Australia, France

ISBN : 978-81-212-6312-2 (PB)
First Published, 1880

2nd Impression 2022

Printed at: Gyan Press, Delhi.

THE SECRET OF A GOOD MEMORY
Author: J. MORTIMER-GRANVILLE

THE SECRET

OF

A GOOD MEMORY.

BY

J. MORTIMER-GRANVILLE.

TO THE READER.

So far as I am aware, no writer on "Mnemonics," or propounder of a formal system of memory, has hitherto recognised the fact that every mind "takes in" and "treasures" the impressions received through one sense-agency — e. g. *sight* or *sound* — with especial readiness; while in "remembering" it employs the same or another sense, mentally or physically, as an agent to recall the impressions previously lodged in the memory.

It is obvious that no success in cultivating the memory can be confidently expected unless the system of training adopted is of a nature to suit individual peculiarities.

The purpose of the following pages is to show how the faculties employed in memory may be tested and their strength or weakness ascertained, so that the method of culture pursued may be in harmony with the law of Nature. Surely the natural way of remembering must be the best.

If it were not abundantly proved by experience, as well as laid down by authority, that "there is nothing new under the sun," I should claim originality for the recognition of certain special use made of sound-phantoms and sight-phantoms respectively in the cerebral work of "taking-in," "treasuring," and "recollecting," as described in the following pages.

However the question of priority may be decided, I will venture to ask the reader's aid in developing the subject, and making it thoroughly practical. To this end, I beg that every one interested in the experiments detailed at pp. 26–32 will send me, under cover to the Publisher of this little book, the first rough papers employed in testing his own powers, and those of any other persons who may take the trouble to make the inquiry. My object will be to determine the relative proportion of sound and sight memories extant.

J. MORTIMER GRANVILLE.

CONTENTS.

WHAT MEMORY IS, AND HOW IT WORKS.

LET us try to get a general notion of what happens when we receive a mind-impression from some object of sight, sound, feeling, or thought, and, taking-in or forming an *idea*, store it in the memory to be "recollected" at future periods either by accident or intention.

When a voice is thrown into the receiving aperture of a phonograph, it sets a disc like a drumhead vibrating. At the back of this disc, and attached to it, is a needle which, with every movement, impresses and indents a sheet of tin-foil spread on a revolving cylinder — that is, each vibration of the disc engraves with the needle a mark on the tin-foil. The forms of these marks or impressions vary with every sound, and, when the cylinder is caused to revolve at such a rate as to move the tin-foil away as fast as it is marked, the result will be a dotted line, which is, in fact, the *writing of a sound.*

The tin-foil thus inscribed will retain indefinitely the impressions it has received. If it be now placed in an instrument so constructed that a needle attached to a musical drum or disc—the reverse of the apparatus just described—shall pass along the tin-foil and be made to vibrate by the marks previously indented or engraved on its surface, this vibration will set the musical disc in motion and produce a series of sounds closely resembling those which first marked the tin-foil.

Hereafter, doubtless, it will be found possible to ascertain the precise character of the marks produced by, and, in their turn, capable of producing, particular sounds. When this is accomplished, cylinders may be engraved with the indentations necessary to cause certain vibrations, and a system of sound or voice writing will be established.

Meanwhile we may notice four points of interest:

1. The phonograph when in motion receives the impression of every sound which is thrown into it; 2. The record is indelible though dormant; 3. The impression received can be reconverted into an expression whenever the cylinder is again set in motion under suitable conditions; 4. What was received as a sound is recorded or retained as a physical record. These facts about the phonograph will serve to illustrate the process of mental-impression and memory.

Brain substance, speaking broadly and in a popular sense but with sufficient accuracy, consists of a multitude of cells or corpuscles or granules of living matter, which are capable of being impressed by mental or nerve force, as the tin-foil on the cylinder of a phonograph is impressed by physical force. Whether these corpuscles are altered in form or state, or simply thrown into special relations with each other when ideas or thoughts are projected upon them, science has not yet been able to ascertain, but that they are in some way physically affected by every mental act is certain.

Whatever we hear, see, or think, produces an impression, wholly irrespective of any consciousness on our part. Attention, and what is called interest in a subject, may deepen the impression produced; but the brain receives the impression of passing thoughts, and of ideas presented to it — even without our knowledge. The record is indelible so long as the corpuscles themselves last, or are capable of reproducing others which shall be the counterpart of themselves in the process of bodily growth and change. A large and healthy brain, well nourished, will take in and register a vast number of ideas, and the records so treasured up constitute the physical bases of memory.

In the process of recollection, mental force — whatever that may be — throws the brain, like the cylinder of the phonograph on which the dented tinfoil is stretched, into a state of activity probably *vibratile*, and the result is a reproduction of the ideas which previously impressed the brain. This is a concise but general account of what occurs when the mind is in action. Now we can compare the two phenomena — sound writing by the phonograph, and thought-recording by the cerebrum — with the consequential processes of reproducing sounds from the dots and lines traced on the tin-foil of a cylinder, and re-collecting thoughts from the altered or specially related corpuscles of brain substance.

It is only while the receiving cylinder of the phonograph revolves that sound impresses it, so to say, *legibly*, and it is only while the brain is in action that impressions of thought are received *consciously*, but all sounds and all perceptions are recorded by the phonograph and the brain respectively. This last-mentioned fact is of high moment in relation to mind and character — which, so far as the mental part of the individuality is concerned, is the formulated expression of mind. The surroundings and collateral influences operating on a mind impress and permanently mark it continuously, whether consciously or unconsciously.

Ideas or thoughts occurring at the same time are generally connected, as though the impressions they produce were recorded on the same tablet or traced on the same sensitive surface; hence what is called the "association of ideas." Some reach the brain through the eye, others through the ear; many — the most completely objective — impress themselves by their various qualities or characteristics through the several senses at the same instant: as when the idea of "wind" forms itself from the sight of bending trees, the sound of the blast, and the feeling it produces of force and cold; the impression being many-sided and produced through the eye, the ear, and the general sensation simultaneously.

The perceptive keenness of the several senses differs with the individual development. Some persons receive impressions more readily through one avenue than by others. This is not unfrequently so much the fact that, even with regard to the reception of ideas presented to their minds in language, they can understand what they read better than what they hear, or the converse; and, although, as above remarked, impressions are received unconsciously as well as consciously, that which is best understood generally makes the clearest, deepest, and therefore the most permanent impression.

It is, however, true that the brain is impressed while the consciousness is inactive, and perhaps also while the attention is diverted; and, when the brain is afterwards thrown into action, it will reproduce ideas which seem quite new, because the mind has no recollection of having previously received them. This explains many strange cases in which persons have been found possessed of knowledge with which they had not previously been credited; and it throws some light on the fact that there is little originality in the world, and that men and women with the most innocent intentions repeat their own ideas and those of other persons, committing obvious plagiarisms unwittingly.

Once lodged in the brain or mind, an impression may lie dormant indefinitely until some discharge of mental force or energy happens to take place through the particular layer, or stratum, of corpuscles which embodies the record of the idea. If the mind has intentionally considered the subject-matter of a particular set of conceptions thus recorded, this act will have created a special chain of connections, or, as it were, laid a train of communications, along which an effort to re-collect or re-cover the idea will travel easily and call it back.

This is how what is, as we say, most "thoroughly learnt" comes to be most easily remembered. It is not impressed more deeply or indelibly than much we have never tried to learn and would gladly forget, but it is specially linked with other ideas by thought and placed ready to be recalled. It is possible to develop this artificial process of "committing to memory," or *preparing to recollect*, too highly, and thereby to prevent the stability of impressions received, as by the method known as "cramming," the recourse of overburdened or hurried students, but a disappointing artifice at best, and one which may easily prove disastrous to the mind which is unnaturally pressed and distressed.

Every one has some special method of his own

for recalling ideas. Some persons, as I have said, *take in* notions of fact best by the ear or by the eye respectively; and the mind afterwards converts the impression thus received into the form most congenial to its sympathies or instincts.

For example, if a man with an acute faculty of hearing, but a preference for thinking by the agency of mental sight, listens to a lecture, he sits with his eyes closed and, unconsciously perhaps, pictures the words he hears as if writing them. Such a person will probably form the connecting links of his ideas by thought-picturing, and when he desires to "remember" what he has heard he will again close his eyes and call up his mind-pictures. The errors into which a mind so working is likely to fall in learning or recollecting will be those proper, so to say, to defective or hurried perception by sight or vision. Another person will convert the impressions he receives by sight into sounds, and probably remember by tone or tune.

It is therefore by no means a necessity that the same mental sense which is used in receiving impressions should be employed in recollecting them; but it generally happens that, if a thought or idea is consciously stored in the mind, it will be recollected by the same mental process that treasured it in the memory—that is, the process or method of thinking for which the mind has a preference.

In sleep mental force, like a weak current of electricity, seems to permeate the substance of the brain without any directing purpose, and the result is a successive awakening of thoughts without order or inter-relation, except such associations as may have been formed in the physical bases of memory by the fact of a particular set of ideas having been impressed on the same surface or tablet, or specially connected by thought, as before explained.

When the mind is intentionally "thinking," thought travels more or less directly in the lines projected by a definitive purpose, and in a well-organized mind calls into action only particular records which, for the most part, it knows where to find. When "thought wanders," because the will is impotent or lacks purpose, and when the volitional consciousness is suspended, as in sleep, the tension of thought is reduced to a minimum, and the force seems to flicker through the accumulated mass of corpuscles, passing at random from layer to layer or stratum to stratum, with the result of inchoate dreams.

"Reverie," and the day-dreaming which characterises, if it does not constitute, certain forms of insanity, is mental wandering of this meaningless sort, which toys with the records of ideation, the bases of memory. The habit of allowing the faculty of thought to wander capriciously through the storehouse of memory and turn over its treasures with no fixed intent—in a word, thinking which is not thinking, but a listless submission to thought—whether the object be to indulge in prurient, to bask in pleasant, or to brood in selfish sorrow over sad and painful, recollections—is one that seriously undermines the authority of the will, and tends to bring about that insubordination of the thinking faculty which first prevents natural sleep, and then destroys reason.

The majority of common-place dreams are simply recollections heaped together without system or method. What coherence they seem to possess is due to the original associations of the ideas which compose them, when these were first impressed on the brain. The subjective experience is very much like turning over a portfolio of pictures illustrating places which have been visited and scenes witnessed. Sometimes the most recent memories are reproduced in sleep, at others the more remote.

The series of records among which thought wanders in sleep will depend chiefly on the general tone and tension of the mind, with this factor in the case, that, if only the consciousness sleeps and the automatic[1] faculty of mental activity remains awake, the latter is likely to go on with the work of the day, and then the worry of dreaming about work or of recent experiences is produced, with all the weariness and irritation this troubling of brain-rest inflicts on the mind and its sense-organs.

The automatic faculty of thought, by which I

[1] See "Sleep," in *Sleep and Sleeplessness.*

mean the lower or inner faculty of reason which carries on the processes of mental work in what physiologists call "unconscious cerebration," is capable of performing very active functions during sleep, and some of its imaginings approach closely to the seeming originality of waking thought. Again, there are many degrees of insensibility in sleep, and in the lighter forms of slumber particular series of thought-records are called into activity by passing impressions of sound and sight — such as the flashing of a light across the closed eyelids — and general sensations like those of cold, heat, or skin-irritation.

Something also is due to position when sleeping. The blood — which is the life — flows more, or less, freely through dependent parts of the body and limbs happening to lie in constrained postures; and this circumstance with its conditions produces particular activities of memory in dreams. Thus a cramped position of the hands may stir that part of the brain which is the seat of those records, or combinations of corpuscles, that constitute the physical bases of dexterity; and a man may dream of his 'prentice days, or of some especial effort in which his skill was peculiarly tested. In this way also the physical disturbance of any organ of the body — as the stomach by food — may induce recollections that compose dreams.

It is not necessary, or even probable, that any record of the past will be produced singly or intact. There is a kaleidoscopic method of throwing the pictures of thought together, so that they form apparently new compositions; and, when we remember that a very large proportion, perhaps the great majority, of the impressions produced on the brain by its surroundings have been taken in unconsciously, it can occasion no surprise that the material of our dreams should seem new.

In these and other processes memory may be studied, and will be found to consist of a simple current of mental force, either projected by the will or wandering in obedience to physical laws unconsciously, along old tracks of connection, or glancing from stratum to stratum in the mass of impressed, or combined, brain corpuscles.

It follows from these general considerations that what we call the mind is not only stored with, but affected by, the multitude of impressions it receives from its surroundings, and that only a small part of the process of brain-marking or registering is under the cognizance and control of the will. Hence the obvious importance of protecting the young from "evil communications" which — since every impressed record may, like the dotted and lined tin-foil of the phonograph, be some day reproduced as an expression — will certainly "corrupt good manners."

What is taken into the mind consciously, and perhaps even that which is taken-in unconsciously, is recast in a particular mould through a special mental sense, instinctively, before it is recorded. It must therefore help the power of recollection to ascertain what this special sense is in each individual experience. The mistakes made in recollecting — for example, in writing from dictation — will often guide to the sense.

Thus, when words of similar sound are commonly substituted for those it is desired to write, probably the mind is accustomed to record its impressions by *sound* in a sort of musical sense, and will perhaps write and think in the rhythm of a particular tune, often one which has much impressed the mind in infancy. From such mistakes as compounding parts of different words together, or dropping members of a sentence, it may be inferred that the mind *pictures* its thoughts; and the method of its recording, and therefore of its recollecting, process will be mental vision.

It is obviously useless to suggest a visual habit of recollection to a man who records and remembers by sound. A rough guess as to which of these two methods any individual adopts may be hazarded by observation of the posture he assumes while thinking, whether he seems to listen as for a sound, or fixes or closes his eyes, to call up a picture-thought. It is, however, necessary to know whether he is at the moment "taking in" an idea or "storing it." The method of recollecting of course agrees with the storing process.

A vivid recollection of particular events or subjects may occur when any special part of the brain, or that organ as a whole, is excited in disease or at a crisis in the physical life — for example, in a moment of drowning, or perhaps some form of death in which the vital flame shoots up for an instant before it finally expires. A blow on the head, producing a general excitement of the faculties, may quicken the memory.

A rational view of memory, wherein it consists, how thoroughly physical it is, and what are the laws that govern its formation and exercise, can scarcely fail to prove helpful at any period of life, and especially in youth. Meanwhile it should be borne in mind, that mere memory is not either a very exalted or an "intellectual" faculty. The lower animals and many idiots excel intelligent men in this quality, the receptive and retentive plasticity of brain.

The highest form of mental efficiency is that which consists in a healthy, co-ordinated, disciplined, and trained development of the faculties a keen intellect may require to employ in excogitating or finding any idea which is needed for the pursuit of knowledge or the performance of a behest of the will.

The intellectual packman, who carries his stock-in-trade with him, is not so high in the scale of mind-growth as the expert and cultivated thinker, who knows where to look for what he wants when it is needed, and possesses the ingenuity necessary to make the largest and best practical use of the comparatively small store of facts and details of "information" with which he cares, or dares, to burden his memory.

Such is a general view of the subject of memory, what it is and how it works. I propose in the following chapter to follow the lines of inquiry here briefly indicated further into detail, with the endeavour to deduce some practical suggestions. To make the matter as plain as possible, it will be necessary to pass more than once over the same ground; but the reader will forgive the repetition[1] if the object is attained. To discover the secret of a good memory must be worth some trouble and pains.

[1] On glancing over the succeeding pages at the moment of going to press, I regret to find there is great need for this apology.—J. M. G.

TAKING-IN AND STORING IDEAS.

THE fact that there is a practical difference between *knowing* a thing and being able to *remember* it is sure to be brought home to the student in any branch of science, or the man of business, very early in his career. What precisely is the nature of this difference, and how is it to be adjusted? Before we try to find answers to these homely but earnest questions, let us expose and put out of the way a source of misconception which often occasions trouble and disappointment to minds admirably fitted for intellectual work, but inexperienced in the exercise of their powers and faculties.

A man of acute and clear perception, endowed with a quick understanding, will comprehend a subject, take it in with a rapid mental glance, and seem to have made it his own. He "learns easily," but, alas! he forgets with even greater facility. The truth is that he has never *learnt* in any mnemonic sense. What he has done is to *apprehend*, and although the brain is undoubtedly capable of a process analogous to instantaneous photographing, it rarely performs this function at the bidding of the will, unless it has been specially trained to do so; or when it does thus instantly receive an impression, the record is not permanent.

The faculty of instantaneous mental photography is more commonly the agent of the sub-consciousness[1] than of the supreme Consciousness, and it takes in the impressions we would gladly have effaced, while those it is desired to retain are obliterated almost as soon as they are registered. Apprehension, or the power of "taking-in" ideas, is a function of the intellect which may be, and in the case of what are called *clever* persons often is, developed to a high degree of efficiency without any corresponding exercise of the "storing" or recording faculty.

[1] See "Habit," in *The Secret of a Clear Head.*

Just as a man may work out a problem, or perform an arithmetical calculation with perfect command of the data and processes involved, but in no way burden his mind with the details, or even the results of his work — if these do not personally concern him — so he may concentrate attention and bring his reasoning faculties to bear on a subject of study, mastering its details and obtaining a clear comprehension of the whole, while he is not registering any impression to form the basis of a "memory."

It is a notable circumstance that in a large class of minds the faculty of apprehension is developed, as it were, at the cost of that of mental registering or memory, the force of the intellect being expended in understanding, while the storing of impressions is left to chance, which generally means that it is neglected.

It is therefore important to bear in mind that a quick understanding does not either involve or imply an aptitude for study. It is simply an effective power of perception, and is not uncommonly associated with a proneness to forget, which is in truth the effect of an absence or inefficiency of the faculty of mental recording.

The distinctness and almost antagonism of these two functions of the mind, "taking-in" and "storing"—or understanding and memory—is curiously apparent in the fact, to which I have previously alluded, that some idiots exhibit extraordinary powers of retention and recollection, while the most intelligent hearers and readers frequently find to their cost that they are the most forgetful. The intelligent student should not allow any consciousness he may have of possessing a quick understanding to encourage him in the neglect to cultivate his memory or be misled by a "good memory" to assume that he is endowed with high intellectual capabilities.

It is, undoubtedly, possible that the mind may be duly charged with a record of any subject or information, and, nevertheless, be unable to recall it at will. This circumstance arises from the fact that memory concerns the *method* of recording rather than the record itself. A piece of knowledge — if I may use the term — is put away safely in the archives of memory, but no care has been taken to mark the place of deposit, or to leave a clue for its recovery when wanted. It may turn up at any moment, but cannot be reproduced by the will, for the simple reason that *will* has not been concerned in putting it away, or is not orderly in its action and trained for the special task of recollection.

The difference between knowing a thing and being able to remember it, is the difference between having property and knowing where to find it. The way to adjust this difference is to make the act of storing impressions a function as well as the processes of receiving and shaping them.

This is what some persons try to do by a recourse to what are known as "techical memories." Those who attach value to these devices must bear with me when I contend that they are not in harmony with the teachings of psychology, and are therefore unscientific. It would be absurd to assert that they are useless, because everyone knows that many a bewildered student has been helped by such expedients; but clumsy and needless tools are often employed in good work and, nevertheless, wisely thrown aside when it is found that the work can be done much better without them.

The natural and only true basis of memory is a well-formed impression. It is not essential that the impression should be fully understood at the time it is made, or the subject-matter wholly mastered by the understanding, but if the record is to be found by thought at pleasure, it must be registered by thought, and in such a way as to be easily recoverable. If the will is to control the act of recovering, it must be directly concerned in that of storing, and it will greatly facilitate the cultivation of a serviceable memory, if the processes of apprehending and recording are studied together and intelligently combined or correlated.

The organ of the mind is, as I have pointed out in the opening chapter, connected by several lines of communication with the external world of fact and suggestion; and impressions — or more accurately the agents of impression — travel with greater facility along some lines than by others. One man will be more effectively impressed by what he hears than by what he sees, and so on. The deepest, clearest, and most permanent impressions are those made when the subject-matter is communicated to the brain by several senses at the same instant, or at least during the same observation.

The impression received from an object that can be seen, heard, felt, and perhaps brought under cognizance by the olfactory sense simultaneously, will be more distinct and lasting than that of another object which can only be recognized by a single perceptive faculty. Nevertheless, most persons have a special aptitude for receiving impressions through some particular avenue of the senses, and it is important for the student to ascertain which is the most open and sensitive of the lines of communication in his individual case.

A simple experiment, which may be described as follows, will, if carefully performed, supply the information desired. Let some person—not the subject of the trial—write on a slip of paper, which we will call No. 1*a*, six or eight familiar words, each consisting of a single syllable, in such order that they shall not have any connections of meaning or sense.

If the number of words suggested should prove too great in any case, a smaller one may be employed, but it is necessary that the words should be arranged so as to avoid the least connection, or the result will be misleading, because the *ideas* will be less in number than the *words*, whereas it is essential that each word should represent an independent and distinct idea. Figures would do as well as words, but that they too readily combine to represent compound ideas, and for our immediate purpose we must use simple ones.

Let the same person next write the same words in a different order on another paper, No. 2*a*, again carefully avoiding any arrangement which might connect the words in thought by sound, sense, or meaning. The person to be experimented upon must neither have seen nor heard the contents of the two papers, or even know the precise number of the words written.

Now place the paper No. 1*a* before the subject of the inquiry, and let him read it *once only*, silently, so that no element of sound may be imported into the experiment. Then remove the paper, and make him at once write down from memory the words just read as nearly as possible in their proper order. This should be done quickly, because the purpose of the experiment is not to test the permanence of the impression, but the readiness and clearness with which it is formed. As soon as he has written all he can recollect, take away the paper, without waiting for any correction or addition, and mark it No. 1*b* for reference hereafter.

Next let the person who wrote the words on paper No. 2*a* read them once, clearly, at an ordinary rate, neither too fast nor too slow, and without any particular emphasis, and let the person to be tested after he has heard the words read, immediately write down what he can remember. This result must be quickly removed with the same precautions as before, to avoid after-thought, and the paper marked No. 2*b*. The process is then to be repeated in an inverse order, the words chosen being different, and the arrangement as heteroge neous as in the first stage of the experiment, bu the oral reading being given first, and the papei which is read at sight subsequently. The paper containing the results should in each instance be marked with the number corresponding to the test paper +*b*.

The two sets of papers are now to be carefully compared, and a judgment formed on the *general accuracy* of the words and their order. If no great difference is apparent in the results obtained, the experiment may be repeated with any variation, such as the substitution of figures for words, but the conditions must be carefully adjusted, so that the memory is not helped, or the burden of the trial will be thrown on the "recollection" instead of on the faculty of "receiving impressions."

It will not generally be difficult to form a clear

notion of difference between the aptitude displayed for receiving by ear and by eye respectively, and the readiest faculty will be the one on which it is safest to rely so far as *taking-in* knowledge is concerned. The man who apprehends most readily by ear should not, as a rule, take notes of what he wishes to remember, at least at the time of hearing a statement, whatever he may do afterwards; while he who is not so expert in receiving notions from the ear as by the eye will do wisely to take down a note in shorthand, or even write a full memorandum, by way of impressing it on his mind. The latter will also probably find that he derives more advantage generally from reading books than from oral instruction, which is in a special degree useful to the learner by ear.

It is, however, necessary to know more than this experiment has, so far, communicated. The faculty of "taking-in" or reception is, as I have said, one thing, that of "storing" or retention another. In order to explore the latter, it will be desirable to repeat the experiment already described with new word materials, and to allow an interval, *say of half an hour*, to elapse between the reading by sight and writing from memory, in the one case, and the same time between the dictation and writing in the other. Great care must be taken to render the intervals as nearly as possible equally distractive as regards the way the mind is employed, and by reversing the order of the sight and sound tests, as previously indicated, to correct any error likely to creep in from the fact that when the same words are brought a second time under cognisance they are, of course, familiar.

This further experiment will throw new light on the comparative efficiency of the two faculties as recording agents, but to obtain the full information required, the four sets of test and result papers must now be examined from another standpoint. The *nature* of the mistakes made is not less suggestive than the relative amount of inaccuracy they display. We have already remarked that as a rule persons who habitually remember by ear — that is, by calling to mind a mental phantom of *sound* —

will, when writing from memory, make mistakes suggested by similarity of sounds; the words written, if not the right ones, will be of somewhat like sound; while specially soft-sounding words or syllables are readily forgotten and omitted. On the other hand, those who remember by pictures of thought or mental characters, are apt to substitute words that bear a general resemblance to each other in their own caligraphy, and to drop words, or parts of words, as though writing hastily from an ideal copy.

Errors of this class are of several kinds. When the recording or the mentally constructive faculty — that is the power or function which corresponds to the faculty used in storing now considered as giving-out — is more acute and rapid in its operations than the muscular activity of the voice-organ in speaking, or the hand in writing, so that in reading the understanding outruns the utterance, or in writing the work of composition goes ahead of the pen — which must generally be the case with intelligent and practised readers or writers — there will be a certain proneness to drop the words in a sentence or the letters in a word.

In original writing and extempore speaking a rapid thinker composes in advance, and copies from memory the ideal phrase he has constructed. The mind, as it were, impresses the words on a scroll which seems to be rolled away as rapidly as it is filled. The higher faculty of thought works in advance; and the automatic faculty is perpetually struggling to transcribe the writing that glides before it, or take down the words sounded in thought.

There is conclusive evidence that the process of copying or writing from dictation is automatically performed; it may even proceed while the Consciousness sleeps. The progress maintained by the mental composer — who, as it were, pushes on his ideas as he forms them in the mind — is frequently too rapid for the mental copyist, and words escape the latter and are omitted from the writing or discourse.

When the difference between the two processes

is very great, the higher faculty has, every now and again, to come to the aid of the lower, which has failed to catch the passing thought. When this happens habitually, the progress of the associated labour is interrupted, and almost any form of mistake or error may ensue.

In an extreme case of this class the condition is identical with that which obtains when a man cannot carry a book in his hand without letting it fall the moment his attention is diverted. The power of automatic action seems to be suspended, or so impaired that it is unable to carry out a process which has been originated by the will, and then relegated to the control of its subordinate agent.[1]

When thought thus outruns the automatic action in writing, usually the later words of a sentence, the final letters of a word, are those dropped.

A practised reader or speaker, as we have before remarked, sees far ahead of the word with which he is immediately engaged. If this were not the

[1] See the paper on "Habit," above cited.

fact, an appropriate inflection of voice would be impossible. It is because children, or adults who are learning to read, or who decipher with difficulty, do not see what lies beyond the word they are construing, their utterance is devoid of emphasis. They cannot tell until the end of a sentence be reached whether it is a question or simple assertion. A diffident but quick reader or speaker, on the contrary, not uncommonly worries himself with the pronunciation of a word some distance in advance of him, and even rehearses it mentally.

When the automatic faculty is not enfeebled, but only slow, it is more common to find sentences and words left unfinished than deficient at the outset; but this rule scarcely holds good in practice, and is of small value in diagnosis, because if the automatic faculty be expert, though tardy, it tries to finish an imperfect sentence or word, and may do this by tacking on the first or last part of a subsequent word or sentence which has been imperfectly recognized while labouring with the earlier.

The principle of these errors may be comprehended by anyone who will make the experiment of transcribing a few sentences written round a drum, which is made to revolve at a fair speed on a vertical axis, from right to left of the observer, and is so covered that one word only can be seen at a glance. The automatic faculty cannot read in advance like the perceptive consciousness. When the perceptive or constructive power is slow or embarrassed in its action, the automatic faculty will sometimes continue to write the word kept standing before it, and either double the word or its letters.

The same result is produced if, as often happens when the thoughts wander, the consciousness repeats itself. Again, in the act of trying back, words clinging to the perceptive faculty are apt to be transposed. This is a common fault, and its cause is nearly always located in the higher consciousness. It can seldom be automatic, as the subordinate faculty either writes, or utters, or drops the word before it. When automatic repetition occurs, that is due to the failure of the higher faculty to remove the copy. If the automatic faculty errs by adding to a word or sentence, it will be by recalling a letter or word already passed, and writing it or speaking it again, but this can only occur when no new word is before it.

A mind wearied with too prolonged work is extremely prone to mistakes of the nature we are now considering. Conscious of the effort it is making, the imagination will compose a whole sentence in advance, and fall into confusion in writing or speaking it. Some transpositions occur in this way, but they are more commonly the effect of thought-wandering than weariness.

A frequent cause of failure in the faculty of attention is striving to think of more than one thing at a time. It is of course *impossible* that the mind should be engaged with two topics at the same instant. The expertness which seems to accomplish this feat is, in fact, a highly developed power of glancing from one subject to another with great rapidity — a sort of mental trapeze-flying wherein the performer often gets an ugly fall, and may be permanently disabled. If he escape this calamity, there will probably come a time when he will discover that he has so impaired the power of application, that he can scarcely follow a long sentence or carry out a sustained process of reasoning.

Those who are compelled by their daily avocations to practise this flying method of thought should for their own sakes make it a rule to read, if possible, aloud — in any case attentively — a chapter or two of some sufficiently engrossing work at short intervals, so as to cultivate the power of sustained and continuous attention.

The habit of composition by a process of sound-conception, gives rise to a special class of errors, in which words or letters having a similar sound are substituted, and then the defects of pronunciation proper to an individual, a dialect, or a language, will predispose to particular mistakes.

For example, *were* or *wear* will be written for *where*, *witch* for *which*, *wen* for *when*, if no difference in these sounds is habitually recognized. The substitution of *is* for *his*, or *er* for *her* is a common misadventure with those who do not aspirate the *h*, or the opposite error may be made by persons who either in jest or habitually sound *h* when that letter is absent. *Knew* for *new* is a frequent blunder, and such substitutions as *cousin* for *cozen*, *not* for *knot*, *rap* for *wrap*, are obviously probable. It would be easy to multiply examples, but these will suffice.[1]

A curious circumstance in connection with this writing or speaking from mental sound is that the individual (unconsciously it may be) composes in a peculiar rhythm, which is often adopted from some verse or song which impressed the mind in infancy. Occasionally the recognition of this rhythm, or tune, will supply the key-note to a character; and, perhaps, without being aware of the circumstance, it is by this suggestion experts in character-reading succeed in making very shrewd guesses as to the leading qualities and habits of a mind from handwriting.

---

[1] Much mischief is done by treating such blunders as trustworthy indications of a special disease. They are *consequences*, not symptoms.

Persons who write or speak from an ideal of sound generally employ the same agent in the operations of memory. This explains the fact before noted, that a man who uses mental sight in this way will gaze intently when he forgets anything, or perhaps close his eyes to avoid distraction, while a person who employs mental sound is more likely to put his finger to his lips, as though to enforce silence, and perhaps incline his head as though listening. I merely mention this in passing.

It will be evident that the facts we have been reviewing supply the strongest possible evidence that it is by a process, which I have elsewhere called mental-reflex, errors of the general classes noticed become habitual. They begin in the sphere of the mental operations by false conceptions and defects in thought-processes, and being reflected in on the brain, they give rise to new combinations, such as those which form the physical bases of memory. They are repeated, and the automatic apparatus develops a special nervous facility for their commission. They then become "habitual" or, which is the same thing, automatic, and beyond the control of the will, which can at best only keep a watchful eye on the way the lesser faculty performs its functions, and correct its mistakes.

By bestowing a few hours on the scrutiny I have suggested (pp. 26–32) any man may obtain a considerable and useful insight into his individual way of taking-in and storing information; and on the basis of the self-knowledge thus acquired he will be able to determine which of his powers he ought to cultivate. This preliminary point being settled, we may proceed to study a few of the most practical methods of developing the faculty it is proposed to train, to the highest attainable excellence, which, of course, will vary with the individual energy, intellectual force, and perseverance.

WAYS OF REMEMBERING.

When a man knows that he takes-in most accurately and remembers with the greatest readiness by *sound*, he should arrange his method of study, so as to work by this faculty directly and chiefly. For example, he ought to be especially attentive in listening, and avoid, as much as possible, being distracted by sounds other than those which convey information. He may read aloud when studying in private, and impress the matters he desires to remember upon his mind by audible repetition, as a child learns his lesson by repeating it over to himself until he knows it. Bearing in mind the need of clues or threads of association by which to recover the matters put away in the brain, he should take care to create for himself in the act of learning a sufficient number of *sound*-links which shall connect the facts he desires to remember, with others.

The various technical formulæ constructed by teachers and recommended to the student fail, first, because they are not the creation of the mind which employs them; second, because they are non-natural and arbitrary; and, third, because the essential difference between a faculty of remembering by *sound* and by *sight* not being recognized, the formulæ adopted are often uncongenial.

Each individual ought to make his own connecting links for ideas, and they should be natural, scientific, and, appropriate to his special faculty. The man who remembers by sound will find it easier and better to recall a fact, event, or circumstance by some formula which connects it by sound than by trying to picture the subject; while the reverse will be the case with the man who remembers by sight. The latter must fancy he sees the object or recall to mind some written or printed description of it before he can remember the details.

The man who is gifted with a memory for sounds

will do wisely to employ that faculty constantly. The voice of a speaker will help him, the sounds of letters, even a sort of musical notation which he will construct for himself intuitively, will contribute to the efficiency of the service sound renders him. The points for him to bear in mind are that in learning, sound-links or connections must be formed, and in "trying to remember" the posture of mind should be one of mental listening, because it is through a *sound*-thought the matter will be brought back to the consciousness.

When, on the other hand, sight is the readiest mode for the reception of impressions, and is also the agent of memory, the aim must be to picture every matter it is desired to remember, either in the shape of an ideal image of the object, or a descriptive record of the subject.

Professors of memory, taking advantage of the large number of persons who remember by mind *imagery*, have developed the system of teaching by pictures to great perfection. With the aid of a few mental images of squares, or outlines more or less simple, they will enable a very dull scholar to "recollect" the most complicated figures and dates, and a seemingly bewildering array of facts. The formula of memory is in all these cases associative, and the lines or spaces employed to fix the several objects of thought stand for the connecting links.

Every way of remembering is, as I have said, a process of link-making, and when a single formula can be made to serve a variety of purposes — acting as the frame for a multitude of pictures — the task is simplified, and the result, for a time at least, proportionally certain. A picture-memory requires that the threads or connecting links by which any subject is to be recovered shall be pictorial; and to make the process natural these links should be, as far as possible, the actual surroundings of the object to be remembered.

There is scarcely any topic which may not be illustrated by figuring of some kind, and the hieroglyphics employed ought to be of the student's own personal devising, except when a teacher has first presented the facts pictorially, in which case it is better to accept and adopt the original imagery, on account of the strength of "first impressions," and the confusion that might be caused by changing symbols.

A common error into which beginners are apt to fall is to try to combine, and therefore confuse, the two methods of remembering—by *sight* and by *sound*. They should be kept carefully apart, and only one adopted—whichever is found to be the most natural and susceptible of culture, in conformity with the law of development, which makes growth and efficiency the fruits of exercise.

A close scrutiny of the results obtained by the experiments I have suggested (pp. 26–32) will show that there is a class of cases in which knowledge is received by one line of communication and remembered by another. The *number* of errors may be greater when writing from sight or sound respectively, while the *nature* of the mistakes made points to the other medium as the agency concerned in remembering!

When this happens, it will be needful to cultivate

the two faculties side by side; but they must not be confounded, and this may seem to create a difficulty. In practice, however, it is easy to make the requisite discrimination, and after the learner has matured his method of study, he will find that the doubling of the process really economises time by improving the quality of the work done.

The feat to be accomplished is simple enough, and bears a close analogy to the procedure of an arithmetician, who "proves" his sum; having added, he subtracts, or the reverse. So the learner by sight who remembers by sound must take in his subject by pictures or characters, and practise reproducing a verbal account of them. If he *hears* most readily but remembers by *sight*, he will do well to listen, and, as I have said, read aloud when studying, then come away, or close his book, and proceed to picture what he has been thinking about, and draw or write a description of the imagery, to impress it permanently. This is what hundreds of persons do unconsciously, and if the process be necessary, in any particular case, it will be found to be natural and easy.

There is nothing novel in these suggestions beyond the recommendation of a formal experiment to ascertain which of the several sense-communications is the most available for practical purposes. All that I have indicated, as being desirable to do, *is* done intuitively by expert scholars; but as intelligent and self-controlled beings, we oûght to know the nature and purpose of every intellectual process we perform, and to young men entering on any career of special study it will be helpful to receive a few hints as to the best mode of procedure.

It does not concern the student standing on the threshold of his work to know in what the physical bases of memory consist—if, indeed, anyone is in a position to give him precise information on the subject—but it is of use to him to be told *how* he remembers, and how to choose the readiest and most effective instrument for the task he has to accomplish.

It is, as I have said, a higher and better thing to possess the power, and know where, to acquire information when it is wanted, than to carry about knowledge as a pack-man bears his burden. At the same time there is so much which it is indispensable every man should learn to hold in his memory, that I venture to offer these few hints as to "ways of remembering."

If the reader has performed the experiment I have suggested, and repeated it, so as to correct or compensate the errors made in working it out, he will be in possession of certain definitive information which is now to form the subject of practical remark.

1. From a study and comparison of the papers marked, at pleasure, 1*b*, 2*b* (pp. 26–31), to distinguish them, written immediately after reading or hearing the words, and looking only to the relative *number* of errors, that is to say, of the words forgotten or mistaken, he will have learnt whether sight or sound is the most open avenue *to* his mind.

2. From the results of the second experiment (p. 32) as shown in the papers — perhaps marked 3*b*, 4*b*, or with some sign to distinguish them from the previous set — *time* being an element in the test,

and the faculty of retention being tried by the lapse of an interval between the reading or dictation and the act of writing from memory, the reader will have further arrived at a judgment as to which of the two classes of impressions is most likely to prove permanent, those entering by the ear, or those presented to the eye.

3. From a careful scrutiny of the *nature* of the mistakes made in the eight, or more, papers, the character of the words dropped, and of those substituted for the original, taking into account the general habit of what is called "forgetfulness," or "inadvertence," but which we have seen to be error or defect in the transcription of a mental copy — an ideal of sound or sight (pp. 31–38) — he will have learnt whether in *remembering* he employs the same agency — sight or sound — as in "taking-in." We have seen that this is by no means constantly the fact. Many, if not most, persons receive most readily one way, and remember another. The *number* of errors made will show the best way of apprehending, the *nature* of the mistakes made in

writing from memory will point to the best way of remembering.

It is necessary in framing any scheme for improving the memory to take both these inferences into account. Subjects or matters which it is desired to store in the mind, must be taken-in by the best means or avenue of impression, and we should arrange to remember them at will by the method which is the most natural, and therefore effective to the individual.

The recognition of these two distinct parts or functions in what is commonly regarded as a single faculty, and called "Memory" has not, so far as I am aware, been made by any previous writer, and I believe it will prove of the highest practical value in an endeavour to cultivate what is certainly one of the most essential qualities of mind-in-action, whether for purposes of learning, business, or the ordinary affairs of life.

Assuming that the reader has mastered the subject thus far and acquired the information to be gained generally by one or two, but certainly by a few experiments, such as I have described, it will now be practicable to discuss the special requirements of distinct classes of subjects, and to set out as briefly as possible the rules by which the aspirant to a good memory should order his procedure and may hope to succeed.

Speaking generally, those matters which are best comprehended by the understanding are longest retained by the memory. That there are many exceptions to this rule, the experience of every scholar must convince him; and, as we have seen, persons of so little intelligence as to be called "Idiots," have often an apt faculty of retention. In short, memory is a mechanical function of the mind, and while it is perfectly true, as men of great intellect have averred, that what is worth remembering, will be retained if it be thoroughly learnt, it is permissible to cultivate the powers of memory by every expedient which will strengthen, or deepen, the impressed record we desire to render indelible, if at the same time the faculties appropriated for receiving and recalling impressions are developed and brought more directly under the control of the will. The defect of most methods which have been devised and employed for improving the memory lies in the fact that while they serve to impress particular subjects on the mind, they do not render the memory as a whole more ready or retentive. The aim must therefore be to develop the natural powers rather than trick them into doing a special service.

To Remember Facts.

If it has been ascertained that the mind takes in most readily by *sound*, any statement of fact, such as a proposition, narrative, or description, which it may be desired to remember, should be heard or repeated with the eyes shut, so as to prevent any needless dispersion of nerve force through the senses during the act of apprehension. This may be done several times. Thus far the process differs in no respect from that adopted by a child when "learning" its lessons. The point on which I insist as a novelty is the observation that the plan of "taking-in" ideas must be specially adapted to the individual peculiarities and the particular mental sense employed.

If it be ascertained by experiment that sight is the most open line of communication to the brain, the method pursued should be to read silently — not even thinking the *sound* of words — and to trust wholly to actual and mental vision for the conception it is desired to make.

In short, the individual whose best faculty for taking-in is sight should use sight only, and in like manner a person who apprehends most readily by sound ought to avoid, as far as possible, trusting to sight. What the sight-receiver has heard he must teach himself by picture-thinking, while the sound-receiver should turn what he has seen into sound, mentally, by rehearsing either audibly or in thought a description of the object which has been presented to him visually.

We now come to the question of "committing to memory," which is an essentially different matter from "taking-in" clearly and rapidly, whether by sight or sound. This is not generally perceived;

and the memory — properly so called — is not exercised. Those who remark that it is increasingly difficult to "learn" in the school-boy sense as we grow older, do not reflect that the exercise of memory by learning lessons is abandoned after the period of student-life, and ever afterwards the adult trusts to the faculty of *apprehension* to keep his memory alive, a misplaced confidence often disappointed, albeit the cause of failure is not, as I have said, generally perceived.

The faculty or agent concerned in the mental phenomenon of recollection, must be ascertained by the experiment detailed at pages 26–32, the mistakes made in recalling a recent record serving to indicate the agent whereby the act of recollection is performed.

If *sound* be the agent or, in other words, if the individual writes from sound-phantoms when writing from memory, the aim of culture must be to develop the faculty of forming phantoms of sound and calling them up at will. It is in this way memory is to be trained and exercised. It will be seen that the object I propose to the reader is to train the faculty of mental sound-making, and to bring it under the control of the will, as a whole, without reference to the special uses to which this faculty may be put. That is a secondary matter, to which we will allude presently. Advocates of the use of "technical memories" err by making the subsidiary purpose relating to a particular use of this faculty the first and only object of attention, with this consequence, that the cultivation of the faculty itself is neglected, and while they can perhaps remember special matters, they cannot attain to a generally "good memory."

To train the faculty of recollection by the use of sound-phantoms, it is necessary to exercise two distinct functions of the mind constantly and with a fixed intention. An individual who has satisfied himself that he writes from sound should make it an hourly habit to think by sound. Subjects which admit of being thought over and "stored" in the mind by noting peculiarities of sound—such as grouping terms under a particular initial letter or musical note-sound—or may be associated by such connecting links as the preponderance of a particular sound or alliteration or rhythm, should be so placed and grouped. Associative sounds are always to be preferred to simply distinctive sounds. When peculiarities of this nature are not easily recognised, it is well to cast the subject of thought into a rhyming jingle. Any person who will take the pains to think this out for himself can have little difficulty in understanding my suggestion, and reducing it to practice. As soon as the habit of sound-making begins to be formed, the experimenter will — if he has not mistaken his faculty — find it perfectly easy to think by sounds, and everything he sees, as well as what he hears, will fall naturally into some niche in the temple of sound which his Consciousness inhabits.

The next step must be to exercise the mind in *finding* and recalling the sound-phantoms it has created and stored in the memory. This is to be accomplished by calling up the sounds previously thought out, and strengthening their connections and making new associations. If the mind is busied with this task for a few weeks, filling every spare moment with the exercise, it will be discovered that it is possible to construct a *mental dictionary of sounds signifying ideas*, so comprehensive and easy of reference that it will in itself constitute "a ready memory."

There is, however, a more precise method of cultivating the faculty of recollection by sound, which may be at once made available for special purposes, and, at the same time, help to strengthen the memory as a whole. This method I will now describe. First let me make an observation which is of considerable moment to the memory-trainer. It matters nothing how an idea is denoted in the category of thoughts. It is the idea itself we wish to fix. In the great majority of instances the original words, in which it may have been embodied when received or formed, will be sounded or pictured to the mind of the person recollecting the idea; but they are of secondary importance, and by laying too great stress on the symbols, or phantoms, of thought, we may commit the mistake of fixing, and afterwards recalling, the words, without the ideas they represent. The best way is to recover the idea by memory and clothe it afresh in words, which, as I have said, are, from association, likely to be those in which it was first received, or re-cast by thought, within the mind.

The recollection of ideas generally may be facilitated by training the faculty by which they are most easily recalled in the manner above indicated, that is, by making the formation of sound-phantoms a habit, and employing every spare moment to summon back and improve the phantoms so formed, at will. To commit to memory and retain at command special facts, the reader may proceed as follows. Form in the mind some tune, rhythm, or series of sounds, which is suggested, or occurs, to the mind at the moment when it is desired to treasure anything in the memory; and first audibly, — then in thought, — intone the matter to be remembered, or enough of it to connect the idea with the tune, rhythm, or sound-series with which it is to be associated. It is better not to connect the subject with any actual or *external* sound occurring at the time, because that cannot be reproduced at desire. If a particular external sound happens to impress the mind at the moment, take advantage of it for the purpose of suggestion, but conceive a similar sound in the mind, so that the association may be wholly under the control of volition. Generally, as I have said, it is enough to form an alliterative line or couplet. If we examine the most commonly remembered sayings and proverbs, it will be found that they are nearly all either alliterative or rhythmical.

Persons with a good ear for music or love of verse will find it easy to commit a whole story to memory by turning it into a doggrel. Sometimes only the first rhyme or cadence can be remembered, but this will generally be sufficient to recall the entire idea. When a subject has been thus "committed to memory," let a few minutes elapse, as though to allow the mould of thought to set. Then recall the subject, and improve the sound-phantom of the thought, connecting it with other sound-phantoms by noting some similarity or difference. Repeat this process five or six times at short intervals, forming new links by comparing the characteristics of the particular sound-phantom which is to form the sign of the new idea, with other sound-phantoms representative of ideas previously lodged in the memory. Each review so conducted will be an act of recollection; and after a few of these efforts of memory have been made, the new symbol, with its attached idea, will become, as it were, fitted into the consciousness, and the physical basis of a *habit* of recollecting it will be formed.

The general effect of this method is, it will be seen, to increase the acquaintance with, and strengthen the control over, previously recorded sound-symbols; and intelligently performed, the exercise is, as it were, a perpetual renewal of old memories. Moreover, there is an involuntary tendency to consolidate as well as deepen impressions, and in process of time the result which experience shows to be gained by concentrating the attention on sounds alone, instead of allowing it to wander amid uncongenial, and—to a mind having a sound-instinct *en rapport* with the memory—unnatural formulæ, will be to reduce the multitude of sound-phantoms to a single series, generally conformable to a simple tune, often, as we have said, one which has been strongly impressed on the mind in infancy.

All this will be achieved unconsciously or without effort, if only the attention be centred on sounds alone, and the individual who has ascertained that he writes from a sound-phantom, will abstain from trying to remember by mental picturing, or sight-phantoms.

When, on the other hand, it is ascertained by experiment that *sight* is the medium by which knowledge can be best attained, and that in writing from memory sight-phantoms or pictures are employed, it is necessary to *picture* everything in the mind, both in receiving and remembering subjects. What is heard must be written or, still better, sketched. Particular facts may be associated with special forms, constituting a system of mental hieroglyphics. Persons possessing this instinct should sketch or write everything, and may freely employ every or any system of memory which consists in *placing* the signs denoting ideas in particular squares or in pictorial relations. Such methods are as useful, because natural, in the case of sight-writers, as they are unsuccessful, because unnatural, in the case of sound-writers. The circumstance that a very large proportion of persons write from sight renders the aids to memory commonly suggested by experts widely useful. The suggestions to be made for the self-culture of writers and speakers from sight-phantoms are identical with those I have just offered for the guidance of sound-writers, except that for sound-phantoms and links of associations the reader must substitute sight-phantoms and connections.

The two classes of persons to which I have already alluded — namely, writers from sound-phantoms and writers from sight or visual phantoms formed in the mind and reproduced in the act of recollecting — may be regarded as pure types; but the multitude of adults do not fall under either description at first, and will only come to enjoy the full advantages of either method after they have finally abandoned that which is found to produce the least satisfactory results on experiment.

Most of us "take in" instinctively by some one natural method, but remember habitually by a process which has been forced upon the mind by bad training or an unwise recourse to empirical aids to memory, which often lend help, although they are not natural.[1] Young persons who desire to acquire full command of the information they possess should, I repeat, avoid the employment of any system which is not either wholly one of sound

[1] I have no desire to say one word in disparagement of the good done, and service rendered, by the authors of special systems of Memory. Their works are well worthy to be consulted, but it is necessary the student should *first* ascertain his own special way of "remembering," and in using the means provided by experts, take care to employ only the formulæ appropriate to his use as a writer from *sound* or a writer from *sight*.

or wholly one of sight, of the particular class and nature proper to their mental constitution.

In seeking the improvement of an adult memory we must take matters as we find them; and this may be done by the following procedure: — First, ascertain the faculty by which ideas are most readily taken-in (pp. 22–29), and employ that solely for purposes of apprehension; but do not trust to it for recollection. Second, ascertain the faculty used in writing from memory (p. 30), and let this only, and always, be the "way" subjects are impressed on the memory and learnt. Third, employ, as far as possible, signs or phantoms which have a double significance, although regarding them exclusively in the sense which agrees with the faculty used in writing, as indicated by the *number* of errors made. For example, suppose a man takes-in most readily by sound, let him listen and imagine sounds in learning, but when he tries to commit to memory for recollection he should employ the method which he commonly employs for memory, as indicated by the *nature* of the errors made.

In my own case, sound is the faculty by which ideas are best received, and the errors I make in writing are nearly always faults originating in confusion of sounds. Nevertheless, I have formed the habit of remembering by sight, having many years ago bestowed a good deal of attention on the system invented by the late Dr. Crook, in which matters to be recollected were placed in squares. I can register and call up to view the several divisions of a thesis by a mind-picture; and recollect what is written by reproducing the sight-phantom of a page. Consequently my memory, though fairly good, is of an impure type, and defective for many purposes.

I am compelled to get over the difficulty by a plan which, in default of a better, I would suggest for the benefit of cripples of my own class — which we are now considering — namely, those in whose mental constitution there is a mixed form of development. It is this: select, for symbols of ideas, arrangements of thought which admit of being mentally recognised by *both* sight and sound. For example, the table of contents at the commencement of this little book will show what I mean. As I am writing these sentences, I remember the topics I have to put under the general head "Ways of Remembering" by two mental impressions which, so far as I can ascertain, are equally strong in my mind. I picture to myself four lines of principal headings for chapters, and between the third and fourth there are six short lines. Thus much the picture — which has been only hurriedly photographed on memory by a hastily made memorandum when I gave the publisher the outline — tells me. Sound helps me to remember the rest, because the first three of these subordinate headings begin with the letter F, and the last three with P. The first series comprises Facts; the second topic I forget; the third was Figures. The second series consists of Persons, Places, Property. I am compelled to refer to the memorandum for the first series, and I find that Figures stands second not third, as I supposed when writing the last sentence. "Forms," the heading I could not recall, just now, but which more than once suggested itself without being recognised, is the third topic, and "Figures" is the second! I account for the mistake by the circumstance that in making out the plan I hesitated whether to place these two last-mentioned headings as they now stand, or to transpose them. This will illustrate what I mean by a memory impaired by the habit of remembering by sight, when sound ought to be the sole agent. It will also serve as an example of symbols fulfilling the requirements of both sight and sound. The order, or place, of these headings forms the pictorial basis for a sight-phantom, which it should be easy to recall; the fact that there are six, composed of two threes, the words in each set commencing with a particular letter, should supply the phantoms for sound.

I will reserve what it is needful to say further in reference to the several uses of sight and sound until the discussion of the other special topics of which I have to treat.

Figures.

There is a specialty in the recollection of figures which it is difficult to understand, but impossible to question. Some persons have a strange, almost amazing, power of remembering numbers and dates, while they seem to have less than the average facility in recollecting other matters. Many individuals, on the contrary, have good memories for ordinary subjects but are unable to "bear in mind" figures of any description. Again, in the course of disease, or decay, it may happen that a man will lose all recollection of dates and numbers, while he still remembers matters of a general character. Taken together these facts point to the conclusion at which the psychologist arrives by another route, namely, that the memory for figures is a faculty almost separate in its exercise, if not distinct in its nature. In any case, it requires special measures for its development.

Speaking generally, I think it may be said that the habitual writer from sound-phantoms is not expert in regard to figures, unless he has intentionally, or compelled by the force of circumstances, bestowed especial thought and care on acquiring a knowledge for which he has no natural love.

To remember figures by sound it is almost always necessary to group them so that it shall be a "combination of sounds" the memory holds and the will tries to recall. This is very remarkable, and accounts for the strange way sound-writers quote and repeat particular phrases, signifying numbers, sums of money, and percentages, all the time being conscious, and not unfrequently giving evident proof, of a lack of power to deal with the data they adduce in argument. As a writer from sound I am painfully conscious of this weakness in nearly every statistical argument in which I engage *viva voce;* and I can generally tell whether my opponent is or is not a sound-writer, by the manner in which he meets me on debatable ground. In short, the peculiarity of mental constitution which determines to the use of sound-phantoms, for the purposes of memory, does not commonly exhibit either a liking or aptitude for figures.

The writer from sound-phantoms will, therefore, do wisely to commit the dates or numbers he desires to keep in mind to the custody of his mental instinct for sound, by throwing them into the form of doggrel or in some way linking the sound of the words denoting the numbers to other words which may stand for the idea with which they are associated. For example, instead of attempting to remember the figures 1815, let him think of the sound expressed by "eighteen hundred and fifteen," and lest this phantom should be confounded with others in his mind, he should connect it in memory with the word "Waterloo" or the phrase "Battle of Waterloo fought in," thus, "Battle of Waterloo fought in eighteen hundred and fifteen." The longer form of words will be recollected with greater ease, because it is more important musically than the shorter, and further, it stands for two ideas, one of which, that of the military action, is represented by two signs, one common, i. e. *fought*, the other specific, i. e. *Waterloo*.

There is another possible clue by which thought

may find the record of a date thus committed to memory. For example, the principal victories won by the British arms may be cast into verse which will go to a tune, the rhythm and cadence marking the order of the words standing for names and dates. In any case the man with a memory, good chiefly for sounds, must use sound-phantoms as the materials of his record, and it will much facilitate his task to link these sounds together, so as to compose a tune or chaunt which he can reproduce mentally. A very simple sing-song will answer every purpose, and he may have as many of these "tunes" or intonations as there are great classes of figure-work which he requires to remember. It is, however, expedient, if not indispensable, that the student should make these formulæ of sound-phantoms for himself. In any case, he must take care to learn them by ear — *the ear of the mind* — and to this end he ought either to compose them without the use of pen and paper, or get some one to read them to him when studying. The caution already given as to the confounding of sound- and sight-phantoms, is especially applicable to the class of persons whose needs we are now considering.

The sight-writer is naturally more at home at figure-work than the sound-writer, and his procedure must be altogether different. The best method, I believe, for those who use sight-phantoms, is to compound the signs by which they remember their ideas as much as possible. A very simple and common plan is to sketch on paper and afterwards picture in space, so as to be able to reproduce it anywhere at will, a large square subdivided into smaller squares like a chessboard, and to place the dates and figures to be remembered in each.[1] This is an admirable process so far as it goes; but when a man has been fancying figures in squares for, say, thirty years, these phantoms are apt to be mixed up, and label them how he will, the wrong square with the wrong figures is likely to be recalled when he tries to recollect.

To obviate this inconvenience, it is better to

[1] Substantially, the method suggested by Dr. Crook.

sketch or picture in the squares thus imagined an outline of some form which shall represent the object: a mental hieroglyphic. If it be required to remember the dates of a king's birth, coronation, and death, picture, in the square proper to denote the order of the reign in the succession of sovereigns, a mental portrait of the monarch, and place the dates under one another on the breast or fore head of the figure, just as the whim strikes the mind. Do the like with *all* the sovereigns, so that the mind may run naturally to the same spot for the information as to each. A very little practice will enable a man to picture the entire *personnel* of a monarchy with its dates, and it will be easy to read the record either way, so as to give the times of birth, of accession, or of death respectively in their order.

The figures will grow so distinct at last that the length of the reign of any sovereign may be ascertained instantly by subtracting the second line of figures, that denoting the date of accession, from the third or lowest line, which represents the date of death. Or the age may be got by subtracting the top or birth line from the last or death line of figures. To fix such a phantom in the memory it is important to recall it frequently and go through the arithmetical processes just indicated. Always connect figures with forms — the forms of the things to which they relate — and put these mental pictures in squares to denote their chronological or successive relations. Subordinate subjects may be placed in lower squares and expressed by less ornate or finished forms, but let every sound-phantom be a complete and firmly sketched picture, with no hesitation or blurring about it, or that will express doubt and cause the remembrance to be indistinct.

It is well to sketch the forms we fancy in the mind. Many teachers lay great stress on drawing or writing everything. I have already insisted strongly on the value of sketching as an adjunct to study, but it is well to work *mentally* when committing a subject to memory. The exercise is good in itself, and develops the faculty of mind-picturing, which it is our aim to train, and the man who so works is independent of place, opportunity, and materials. Those who can only remember by writing or drawing with material appliances are at a serious disadvantage in ordinary life; and the habit of dependence ought not to be formed. Everything should be pictured by the sight-writer[1] with sight-phantoms, and the form should represent the object with which the date or number to be remembered is associated; every article being, so to say, marked in plain figures with its price or statistical value, and hung up in its square. If the mind does not take readily to the use of squares, any other frame will do, but it must be so subdivided as to admit of placing many sets of figures in their natural relations, thus creating links and connections of thought. It is not enough to fancy a number or date in a particular square, there must be a reason for the selection of that position; either it comes in chronological order or it is above or below something

[1] I have used the term "writer" throughout solely because the experiments described at pp. 26–32 were made by writing.

else. Some persons who use squares or compartments and lines in this way, are too apt to forget the constructional value of the phantom picture-frame itself, and so heap together the records they make in a particular place that it is surprising they ever succeed in eliminating a correct number or date from the lumber of figure-phantoms.

We come next to consider

Forms.

At the first blush of the matter it would seem that forms could not be treasured in memory by *sound*-phantoms. It is true that writers from sound are not, as a rule, good at remembering faces or anything depending directly or chiefly on form. Such thinkers make strange mistakes, forgetting and confounding persons and, though in a lesser degree perhaps, places. Nevertheless, it is possible to overcome the difficulty. The device I am about to suggest will seem simple, but it is successful; namely, to endow the forms it is especially desired to remember with motion and sound. These two qualities, motion and sound, are very closely associated. They combine to express life, in which all are interested.

When it is required to commit any form to a *sound*-memory, the course pursued should be to give the form sound by associating it with words, noise, or an expression which shall betoken life. Sometimes it is sufficient to commit the name of the object to memory, with some short verbal description of it, but when it is practicable, sound should always be connected in a natural way with the form: as the tones of a voice or the words of an utterance, with the form of a man; the cry of an animal with its aspect; or a remark made, in connection with a picture or scene. The sound-phantom will constitute a convenient link by which to treasure the form in the memory and recall it at will. It is possible in this way to commit even a complicated pattern to memory, although the individual has no eye for colour or form.

To the sight-writer form is especially congenial as a memory-phantom. It is, in fact, the basis of every record he makes. Nothing needs to be said on this subject by way of suggestion for his instruction, except that it will be wise to cultivate the faculty of mind-picturing without either manual drawing or writing. A person who desires to command a good working memory ought to render his method as purely mental as possible. Although he may, and should, sketch and write as freely as possible, when compelled to "take-in" by sound, in his own study and at all times and places, when committing to memory, the process should be wholly mental. Again, the simplest and most distinctive signs will be most useful, and ideas should be connected by every contrivance in picture-making, so that all it is desired to remember about a subject may be brought before the mind's eye by a single effort. It is a mistake to crowd the chambers of imagery with sight-phantoms which are neither assorted nor grouped for ready reference. The sight-writer should spend his leisure moments in his mental picture gallery, observing, comparing, and cataloguing his treasures.

The three remaining topics falling under the general head "Ways of Remembering," have been incidentally mentioned in treating of the previous subjects. It will therefore suffice to notice the salient errors to be avoided in regard to these, and offer a few general suggestions.

Persons.

The sound-writer will remember persons by their voices and utterances, or by remarks he has heard made upon them, rather than by their forms or features. *Expression* as a subject of memory, is as intimately associated with the words as with the aspect of a speaker, and may be readily recalled by sound. Expression will in its turn help to recall form, but sounds should be made the base of the record. Try to remember a person as he appeared when saying something or being addressed by somebody. In this way the phantom may be most readily fixed in the memory and recalled to the mind of a sound-writer. The sight-writer will, of course, picture in thought, and by an effort at any time reproduce, the semblance of the form.

Places.

The recollection of places — a different matter from that which has been termed the "topographical instinct," wherby an individual will find his way over ground he has not previously traversed — is not so exclusively a sight-subject as it may appear to be. There are many associations of sound by which places may be easily remembered; for example, a cathedral by the sound of an anthem, a place of assembly by a lecture, or a spot on the sea-shore by the sound of the waves and wind, or a farm-yard by the noise of poultry, or any place by the barking or whining of a dog. These are simply illustrations which my own memory supplies, but they will serve to show my meaning. The sound-writer who forms a habit of remembering by sound, will be ever on the alert to connect sound with places, and he will find it far easier to retain and recall memories in this way than by any other. The writer from sight-phantoms is of course at home amid objects which admit of being fixed in the mind by a simple process of mental picturing; but it is especially necessary that a person so gifted should be careful to make ideal copies for his gallery of thought. No amount of gazing at objects will impress them permanently on the memory unless a mental photograph, so to say, be taken and examined again and again until it becomes thoroughly stored in the mind.

Property.

To remember each article among the belongings of personal life, whether keys, papers, books, or implements of work or pleasure, and to know where to find it when wanted, is a task of considerable practical difficulty, not so much on account of the complexity of the feat to be performed, as the want of method which commonly prevails in life and business, and the fact that it is scarcely ever possible to recall the place of a lost article by any natural association. Even with those who begin wisely and have "a place for everything," it can hardly be secured that everything shall be in "its proper place" when wanted. It is easy to remember the places allotted to particular objects, but there is a habit of putting things out of hand when we have done with them, and forgetting afterwards to return them to their proper places.

The most direct remedy for this evil is to create a new habit of making the act of putting articles such as keys, papers and books out of the hand, a more important matter than taking them up! Bestow special thought on the *placing* of objects. Let the sound-writer notice the sound made by the act of placing, and think of its cause. It is not difficult, nor does it tax the attention inconveniently to do this when the habit is once formed. For example, the rattle of a bunch of keys on wood, in a basket, among papers, on a wooden table or a stone shelf, will be different under the different circumstances. If every act of the kind be noticed, when the keys are missed, it will be easy to recall the fact that they were placed with a particular accompaniment of sound, and the place will then suggest itself. It is only by making it an automatic habit of the self-consciousness to note thee asssociations ,of sound they can be rendered useful as links and clues by which to recover a lost object.

The sight-writer should do the same thing with objects of sight. He may form a special habit of noticing the surroundings amidst which he places any and every article, and of particularly observing its appearance when deposited, or some visual fact, such as the turning of a leaf, or the tearing or crumpling of a paper. To this habit, as to every other habit of thought which the sight-writer forms, or cultivates, in aid of his memory, should be annexed the practice of making a mental picture of the object as it is left. All this will seem laborious at first, but the attention, which may without any serious effort be given to the matter for a few weeks, will effect a vast change in the habits of thought and wonderfully improve the memory, besides giving to life as a whole that method without which everything like order is irksome, and the care of details a continuous pain.

I have been desirous to avoid giving specific directions for the detailed steps of these several "ways of remembering," because I am convinced it is far better the student or self-trainer should work out the suggestions submitted in his own fashion.

THE SECRET OF A GOOD MEMORY.

The secret consists in ascertaining the nature of the process by which thought makes its records, and the Will must recall them. It is useless trying to remember by sound if the memory has been made by picture; or the reverse. The experiments detailed at pages 26–32, will, if repeated, at intervals, so as to correct accidental errors of act or inference, enable the reader to possess himself of the fundamental knowledge indispensable to intelligent self-culture.

Being once acquainted with the faculty which is likely to be most serviceable in his enterprise of improvement, it remains to cultivate it. How this is to be accomplished he will learn from the remarks offered in the preceding chapters. I do not think he will need to have recourse to special formulæ for the recollection of particular matters; but if he should find it necessary to do so, the knowledge that sight or sound respectively are his specialties of memory, will enable him to make a wise selection of the most congenial methods. The points to bear in mind are: *First*, that a sound-writer must habituate himself to the creation of phantoms or conceptions of sound embodying or expressing to his own mind, as simply as possible, the facts, figures, forms, persons, places, or property, he wishes to remember. *Second*, the connecting links and associations by which he classes and as it were ties together his thoughts, must also be sound-links, and, as I have pointed out, they should be arbitrary mental links, that is to say, such sounds as can be called up readily by the mind, and which do not require a man to go to a particular place or hear a particular sound to "call to mind" the subject he desires to be able to remember anywhere and at any time instantly.

The same is true of sight. A man who employs sight-phantoms should be careful that they are thought-pictures, so that thought may have them always at its disposal. It is vain to make any act, posture, or condition of the body, the link or connection by which a matter is to be remembered. Memory should be *self-contained.* We all remember the story of the scholar who learned his lesson while playing with a particular button, and could "repeat" it — because it was recalled — by again playing with the same button, and how, when the button was surreptitiously cut off, he could not say his lesson, and stood confessed as a trickster. This is what persons who rely on "technical memories" must be, unless their artificial aids to memory are self-created phantoms of sight or sound stored in the mind and independent of the surroundings.

Artificial formulæ for the recollection of special subjects should always be made by the person using them; and it is desirable that he should construct them in thought only, whether by sound or sight. They ought to be very simple, and if the matter itself does not at once suggest a phantom, it is better to employ one which already exists in the mind, and with which the new idea can be compared or contrasted; the new remembrance will then help others. Above all things, the mental signs for thought should be simple and natural, that the mind may not be worried or bewildered by the burdens imposed on it.

To fix a subject of memory in the mind, whether it be recorded by sight or sound, the record should be repeatedly recalled and remembered. Do this at short intervals five or six times within a few hours of first charging the memory with the subject, and improve, without radically changing, the conception first formed of it. Comparing, contrasting, or classing it with the older phantoms of memory will greatly help to deepen and strengthen the first impression.

To attain a good memory, that is a power of instantly remembering anything at will, give the mind abundant exercise in its leisure moments by recalling and again picturing, or re-sounding, in thought the phantoms it has previously received. By going over and over again the same lines, it is easy to strengthen the memory as a whole and to impress particular subjects very deeply. Besides, by this exercise the mind comes to know the weak points in its stock of knowledge, and can repair defects and replace lost impressions at its convenience, instead of making the discovery of obliterations at moments when it is perhaps of vital importance they should be reproduced. The pains taken in this way will be amply requited.

Knowledge recalled without the aid of books or again applying to sources of external information is far more deeply and permanently impressed than by any act of repetition which is not purely mental. One exercise of memory in this way, the effort being made without extraneous assistance, and by the agency of the particular mind-sense, of sight or sound, which happens to be proper to the individual, is worth many acts of hearing again or reading again; which exercises concern the function of "taking-in" rather than that of "committing to memory." Still less do they relate to the act of recalling the subjects of memory. It is important that the essential difference of these stages in the process of acquiring and retaining knowledge, should be clearly understood.

The familiar saying, "what goes in at one ear goes out at the other," accidentally expresses an important fact, namely, that the agent or instrument of an impression is something wholly apart from the impression itself. It is the stamp, and bears the graven form of a record; but unless it leaves its impress on the brain, no memory can be retained. I said at the outset that *all* sounds and sights and feelings impressed the mind and influenced the character, whether for good or evil. That is strictly true, but the impressions made by unobserved agencies and events are generally blurred and indistinct. In any case they are not under the control of the will, because the will has not been concerned in their production. It is not enough that a piece of information should go in by the ear; if it is to be retained it must be appropriated by the mind, and, as it were, manipulated to a shape consonant with the mental habits of the individual.

To some extent, as we have seen, this process will consist in the transposition of the subject from sound to sight, or the reverse, according to the mental preference; but more than this is involved in the act the mind performs when appropriating knowledge. Thinking over, or studying a subject in thought, is like examining a hitherto unknown object with curiosity and the desire to become acquainted with it. We know what this means in ordinary life, a corresponding exercise should be performed by the mind when a new fact or subject is brought under its cognisance.

Much depends on the way this business is accomplished. If the mind scrutinises every point carefully, and in thought compares it with standards of excellence treasured in memory, the new subject will be deeply impressed, and the record will remain indelible. If, on the other hand, the mind does not take the trouble to go over every little feature of the fact or inference before it, the impression left will be superficial and liable to be effaced. Something depends on the sharpness and depth of the graven image from which the impression has been received, but even more is determined by the earnestness which the intellect bestows on the task of "committing to memory."

A common mistake is that of finding an excuse for carelessness in the matter of appropriating knowledge, or committing information to memory, in the circumstance that the subject-matter of an impression is not "understood." No doubt it is easier and better to comprehend what we learn; but the best informed persons are those who have the most diligent and highly-cultivated powers of *observation*, not necessarily the clearest or most acute faculties of comprehension. Moreover, it must often happen that facts and subjects of great value fall under notice at moments when the mind is not looking for them, or, in an educational sense, ready to receive them. A man may collect materials and hoard them carefully before he has occasion for their use, or is even able to estimate their worth. A well-trained mind will be provided with the power of appropriating all that comes in its way, and storing it for future use, without being compelled at the moment to understand what it commits to memory. The young should be especially careful to cultivate this power, because it will often happen that they are required to learn what they do not comprehend, and if it is not possible for them to do this, in after years they are sure to regret the want of crude material to work upon.

"Committing to memory" is seizing upon the impression produced by sight or sound, and so reviewing and deepening the record made as to render it permanent. Sometimes this can be done by repeating the act of impression, as in repeating or reading a passage again and again in "learning" it; but the most effectual method of accomplishing the object is to revert *several times*, at short intervals, to the subject, and, recalling the impression left on the mind, to re-examine and deepen it by a mental act, without, unless it is absolutely necessary, referring to the original source of the impression, that is the book or object from which the sound- or sight-phantom was derived.

Re-collecting is the act of calling up a brain- or mind-record at will. Obviously, it is impossible to recall what we have not consciously put away. The subjects of memory which have not been appropriated by the will *knowingly*, cannot be summoned at pleasure, although they are apt to come back unbidden. Perhaps little more than half the stock of materials treasured in the memory is under the control of the will. The aim of the intelligent thinker should be to bring his whole mind into subjection to the authority of the judgment. If this were the purpose of all self-culture, there would be fewer lunatics in the world, and not half so many dreamers of dreams full of tumultuous thought.

A well-ordered mind is one with its faculties held under discipline, and its pictures and records of thought systematically arranged, and so placed and connected among themselves as to be easily found when required.

The way to improve a bad memory is to set resolutely about the task of "taking stock" of what has been learnt and is supposed to be known. A strong will can find little difficulty in reducing the chaos of a neglected mind to something like order. This is one of the first enterprises in which those who have bad memories should engage.

The subject is by no means exhausted. It has barely been practicable to do more than indicate the leading lines of study to be pursued, but enough has been said to show the importance of proceeding from a definite start-point and with a set purpose, in the enterprise of self-improvement, and in this I believe the secret of a good memory will be found mainly to consist.

END.

"PANSY" BOOKS.

Probably no living author has exerted an influence upon the American people at large, at all comparable with Pansy's. Thousands upon thousands of families read her books every week, and the effect in the direction of right feeling, right thinking, and right living is incalculable.

Each volume 12mo. Cloth. Price, $1.50.

FOUR GIRLS AT CHAUTAUQUA.
CHAUTAUQUA GIRLS AT HOME.
RUTH ERSKINE'S CROSSES.
ESTER RIED.
JULIA RIED.
KING'S DAUGHTER.
WISE AND OTHERWISE.
ESTER RIED "YET SPEAKING."
LINKS IN REBECCA'S LIFE.
FROM DIFFERENT STANDPOINTS.
THREE PEOPLE.
HOUSEHOLD PUZZLES.
MODERN PROPHETS.
ECHOING AND RE-ECHOING.
THOSE BOYS.
THE RANDOLPHS.
TIP LEWIS.
SIDNEY MARTIN'S CHRISTMAS.
DIVERS WOMEN.
A NEW GRAFT.
THE POCKET MEASURE.
MRS. SOLOMON SMITH.
THE HALL IN THE GROVE.
MAN OF THE HOUSE.
AN ENDLESS CHAIN.

Each volume 12mo. Cloth. Price, $1.25.

CUNNING WORKMEN.
GRANDPA'S DARLING.
MRS. DEAN'S WAY.
DR. DEAN'S WAY.
MISS PRISCILLA HUNTER and MY DAUGHTER SUSAN.
WHAT SHE SAID and PEOPLE WHO HAVEN'T TIME.

Each volume 16mo. Cloth. Price, $1.00.

NEXT THINGS.
PANSY SCRAP BOOK.
FIVE FRIENDS.
MRS. HARRY HARPER'S AWAKENING.
NEW YEAR'S TANGLES.
SOME YOUNG HEROINES.

Each volume 16mo. Cloth. Price, $.75.

GETTING AHEAD.
TWO BOYS.
SIX LITTLE GIRLS.
PANSIES.
THAT BOY BOB.
JESSIE WELLS.
DOCIA'S JOURNAL.
HELEN LESTER.
BERNIE'S WHITE CHICKEN.
MARY BURTON ABROAD.
SIDE BY SIDE. Price, $.60.

The Little Pansy Series, 10 vols. Boards, $3.00. Cloth, $4.00

Mother's Boys and Girls' Library, 12 vols. Quarto Boards, $3.00

Pansy Primary Library, 30 vol. Cloth. Price, $7.50.

Half Hour Library. Octavo, 8 vols. Price, $3.20.

NEW PUBLICATIONS.

THE TEMPLE REBUILT. By Frederick R. Abbe. Boston: D. Lothrop & Co. Price $1.25. A new edition of this poem, re-written, enlarged and rearranged, has been brought out in obedience to a demand on the part of the public, and will be found by those who now read it for the first time a work of high purpose and rare ability. Mr. Abbe is a poet in the truest sense of the word, and his subject is one which gives the largest opportunity for thought and expression. The poem involves the story of primal innocence, the fall of the soul, its restoration through Divine grace, and final salvation. By the "temple" the author typifies the soul of man; it is cast into ruins by sin; the new foundation is the plan of salvation as laid down by Christ; the builders are the Christian virtues and graces; the implements are prayer and good works: and through these the edifice again arises in its pristine purity and beauty. The author paints in vivid language the various scenes which rise before him during the progress of the poem; the bright radiance of the heavenly courts; the thronging seraphim and white-robed angels; the star-gemmed skies; the beautiful things of earth; the horrors of the pit, and the terrible scenes of the last day. The closing portion of the poem is entitled "Hallelujah," and is a call to all created things on earth and in heaven to praise the Lord for his redemption. We quote briefly from this section to give the reader an idea of the characteristics of the author's style and an example of his skill in the choice and use of language:

> Praise Him, ye mountains! on whose beetling crags
> Nestle the eagles, peering for their prey;
> Where from the clouds of thunder tempests bind
> Their brows with terror, and the sullen snows
> With cold caressing lap the traveler;
> Or where the molten entrails vomit fire
> In furious miniature of final doom.
> In higher grandeur yet will you arise,
> Under a fairer sky, a calmer clime,
> Bright pillars of the sun; your radiant brows,
> Disarmed of every weapon of dismay,
> The purple pavement of angelic feet,
> With sovereign peace on every peak enthroned.

The volume is handsomely printed on good paper, and bound in cloth.

NEW PUBLICATIONS.

FIELD, WOOD, AND MEADOW RAMBLES, or How we Went Bird's-nesting. By Amanda B. Harris. Illustrated by George F. Barnes. Boston: D. Lothrop & Co. Price $2.00. Equal in elegance and excellence to any publication of the season is *Field, Wood, and Meadow Rambles*, by Amanda B. Harris. In it the author describes the adventures and experiences of two young ladies who spent one summer in searching the fields and woods for the purpose of studying the peculiarities and habits of the birds of the region. The story is delightfully told, and will undoubtedly rouse scores of young ladies to attempt the same thing next season. The work is illustrated by twelve exquisite drawings by George F. Barnes, with frontispiece, title page and vignette. The paper on which the text and illustrations are printed is of the best; the margins are liberal and the binding elegant and strong. Within and without its attractions entitle it to a foremost place among the best gift books of the year.

LEADING MEN OF JAPAN. With a Historical Summary of the Empire. By Charles Lanman. Boston: D. Lothrop & Co. Price $2.00. No man is better qualified to write upon Japanese subjects than Mr. Lanman, who for several years was a resident of the Empire, and a student of its political, social, and religious elements and characteristics. During the past dozen years Japan has taken immense strides in what we are pleased to call civilization. The customs and beliefs of many centuries have been overthrown; the form of government has been changed, and methods which have until now been peculiar to western nations have been introduced. It is not to be supposed that all this has been accomplished without effort. The men who have played the rôle of reformers have had many obstacles to contend with, and even now there is no lack of opposition to the introduction of foreign civilization. Mr. Lanman gives an interesting account of the changes made, and of the prospects for the future, in these sketches of the leading men of the country. It is a book which every one who wishes to keep abreast with the times ought to read, and which a great many will read. It is the only work of the kind which has ever been published.